# DOS Programming Success in a Day

### By Sam Key

## Beginners' Guide to Fast, Easy and Efficient Learning of DOS Programming

# Table of Contents

# Introduction

I want to thank you and congratulate you for purchasing the book, **DOS Programming Success in a Day:** *Beginner's Guide to Fast, Easy and Efficient Learning of DOS Programming.*

This book contains proven steps and strategies on how to program using the DOS system.

Many people nowadays overlook DOS as a programming platform, but if you use Windows on a daily basis, you will find its capabilities an immense help in completing several tasks. Also, DOS is the perfect place to start learning the intricacies of computer programming -- it is very simple and efficient, and one can easily create useful outputs. If you are simply interested in other kinds programming or if you would just like to learn a new computer platform then this book is for you.

Even before most of the famed programming languages were created, there already was DOS. Several programming languages even owe their existence to DOS as they have been fathered by programmers who initially used DOS to create various programs that served as the backbone of the prototype of several applications oft used by people and organizations. While it is true that DOS is rarely used these days, learning how to program using this old language can help you gain a better understanding of the modern programming languages used today.

With that, thanks again for purchasing this book and I hope you enjoy it!

# Chapter 1: Starting Out in DOS

When people hear the word "DOS" (if they even hear it these days), the first thing that comes to mind is usually the 8-bit graphics that displays a white text on a black terminal that was common back in the days. People tend to equate DOS with the early versions of the Windows OS, and with good reason -- Microsoft's rendition of the system dominated the PC market between 1981 and 1995, the exact same period of time when DOS was one of the most popular computer languages.

The acronym "DOS" stands for "disk operating system," and can refer to any of the many operating systems that can be operated through the command line, which will be discussed extensively in the next chapter. The different DOS-family variants that went up over the years (with many surviving until now) are MS-DOS, DR-DOS, PC DOS, PTS-DOS, ROM-DOS, and FreeDOS. Even some of the GUI Windows OS's until the year 2000 (Win 95, 98, and ME) are partially DOS-based.

Despite the intense competition between operating systems and the general decline of DOS in favor of more advanced systems, some computer manufacturers still used FreeDOS as OEM (original equipment manufacturer). Different devices such as DSLR cameras use a variant of DOS as an embedded system, leveraging its ability to access hardware directly. For gamers, DOS also allows them to run legacy games such as Doom and King's Quest. Since modern operating systems are no longer compatible with DOS, emulators are used to simulate a DOS-compatible environment.

### Why is DOS Programming still important?

DOS started losing its popularity among PC users when it was no longer required by the latest Windows editions; however, DOS programming still carries its own advantages including:

1. DOS commands are very simple to remember mainly due to DOS being a very stable operating system on its own.

2. It does not take a lot of space on the hard drive, allowing those who have older or slower systems to work with it at near-native speeds. In

fact, an entire DOS can be contained in a single modern ROM chip!

3. It has one of the fastest boot times almost across any system. This speed also allows DOS to have direct access over any hardware.

4. It can help resolve issues such as crashed drives; DOS can even format and run old DOS applications.

5. Using DOS allows a programmer to create special-purpose programs that do not require heavy use of graphics.

Despite its simplicity, DOS allows a programmer to control and process the information encoded to the computer. This allows him to access, store, retrieve and translate different files.

# Chapter 2: The DOS Command Line

The most important functions of DOS can be accessed with the use of the DOS Command Line. The command line allows users to input coded instructions using syntax conventions that will be interpreted by a resident program often-referred at as the command interpreter. Every input and output is generated through the command line.

Every line is deemed executable after the user presses the ENTER keystroke. DOS has three known command interpreters and each of them has their own separate list of commands. These three interpreters are:

DEBUG.EXE      This interpreter deals with command files that are sent using input redirection.

COMMAND.COM      This interpreter loads commands that are installed in the computer's memory. Simply, this interpreter is responsible for commands that are already in the computer system with or without DOS installed.

IO.SYS      This interpreter deals with the commands that are included in the general configuration of a particular DOS version.

Each command line can address several commands at the same time but all data inputs must have a specific address enough to identify the input and perform necessary operations based on the instructions coded by the programmer. In other words, no two commands have the same names. The same can be said for files and directories especially if the contents vary.

The name of the objects identified in the command line must be unique so that the computer and the programmer will only have a single understanding of the command. Commands follow specific syntax rules; they are used to manage specific pieces of information, parameters and references to reach a singular definition of the command instruction.

Internal commands, ports and other objects can't be abbreviated nor defined as a variable. These words already have predefined meanings and can't be use to contain data or information in any form.

## Reserved Words

Internal commands are represented by specific names part of the interpreter's command list. They are pre-existing and pre-defined in the interpreter's processing mechanism; therefore, programmers can't use these words for a different purpose other than what's already defined.

Reserved words are not only limited to internal commands as they can include device names in the PC. These names can be used as sources for data manipulation, examples of which are:

PRN        Primary parallel port similar to LPT1

NUL        Void virtual port

LPT1       Primary parallel port

CON        Primary Console
(ex. Display (output); keyboard, mouse, touchpad (input))

COM2       Secondary serial port

COM1       Primary serial port similar to AUX

AUX        Primary serial port

Other device names that are considered reserved are LPT2, LPT3, CLOCK$, CONFIG$, COM3 and COM4. These drivers are part of the DOS core.

## Names

Naming files and directories (regardless if they are ordinary or executable) are required operations in DOS. Names in DOS are limited to just eight characters. If this does not suffice, DOS allows programmers to append the name with a suffix with a maximum of three characters. The filename and its suffix are separated by a dot.

Names and their corresponding suffixes can be made up of letters, numbers and symbols that do not have other reserved functions. Never use these symbols (as they are used to parse command lines):

| | |
|---|---|
| Ampersand | & |
| Dollar sign | $ |
| Exclamation Mark | _ |
| Minus | − |
| Number sign | # |
| Underscore | ! |

DOS does not discriminate between upper and lower case letters except when used in comparative commands like FIND, IF, and SEARCH. With the dot (.) separating the filename and the suffix, that too can't be used in filenames. Other symbols that you should leave out when creating filenames are:

| | |
|---|---|
| Asterisk | * |
| Backslash | \ |
| Colon | : |
| Comma | , |
| Double quotes | '' |
| Equality symbol | = |
| Left arrow | < |
| Pipe | \| |
| Plus | + |
| Question mark | ? |
| Right arrow | > |
| Semicolon | ; |

Slash                                   /

Directories have no suffixes. Most suffixes indicate the file's origin making it easy for you to organize your files. COMMAND.COM recognizes the predefined functions of three special suffixes – EXE, BAT and COM so make sure that none of your files or directories use any of these.

Other suffixes that have predefined roles are:

| | |
|---|---|
| BAK | Archived files |
| BAT | Batch files |
| BMP | Bit-Map-Picture; image file |
| SCR | Command lines source |
| RAR | Compressed executable file |
| ZIP | Compressed executable file |
| CAB | Compressed version of a file; software |
| DLL | Dynamically Linked Library |
| BIN | Executable file |
| COM | Executable file |
| EXE | Executable file |
| EXT | Extension file |
| HTM | File containing HTML |
| INI | File containing resetting information |
| GIF | Graphic Image File; image file |
| JPG | JPEG; image file |
| CPI | Library file containing data for fonts |

| | |
|---|---|
| DAT | Non-textual file |
| RTF | Rich Text Format |
| SYS | System file |
| TMP | Temporary file |
| DOC | Textual file |
| TXT | Unprocessed textual file |

## Paths

Just like real property with addresses, files have paths or their exact placement within a specified directory. Directories are arranged in a hierarchical structure where higher-level directories can contain both files and lower-level directories otherwise known as subdirectories.

Command interpreters use the pathname (determined by the path structure) to easily-locate your file. Here is how a pathname looks like:

```
C:\DOS\MS\Sample.exe
```

In this example,

| | |
|---|---|
| Sample.exe | File being located |
| C:\DOS\MS\ | Directories and subdirectories that leads to the file. |

If a pathname is terminated by a backslash "\", the interpreters ignore the command due to the lack of a target file. The only time DOS interpreters recognize a pathname terminated by a backslash is if it pertains to the root directory. To illustrate:

| | |
|---|---|
| A:\MS\Sample.txt | Recognized |
| A:\MS\ | Ignored |
| A:\ | Recognized |

## Dots

Using dots in DOS can be tricky but all you have to remember is that it symbolizes the current directory as a jump off point. For instance, if you are currently in the `A:\` directory, then

`A:\ABC\handsome.gif`

is the same as:

`.\ABC\handsome.gif`

Interpreters return pathnames terminated by a backslash deeming the path name as invalid. One way to solve circumvent this is by appending a dot to the filename. For instance, if you are trying to open

`B:\COR\LOVE\`

you can try adding a dot:

`B:\COR\LOVE\.`

to get the interpreter to recognize the directory specification.

Dot-dot or double dot ( . . ) is recognized by the interpreter as an alias akin to the root directory. For instance:

`A:\ABC\DE4\..`

is equivalent to:

`A:\ABC`

## Separation Symbols

The following symbols are used to separate words in the command line:

Comma                                   ,

Equality symbol                    =

semicolon                           ;

Space

Among these four symbols, space is the most frequently-used separators. When using the commands `IF` and `SET`, the equality sign can't be used for separation. When using the `ECHO` command, you can't use comma, equality symbol and semicolon as a separator.

When using the PATH command, semicolon plays a special role.

## Slash

DOS uses slash (/) to signal a parameter. For instance:

```
COPY C:\DOS\TEMP\Signal.gif /M
```

The slash tells the interpreter that letter M will be used as a parameter to display a prompt that determines whether the file contained in the TEMP directory should be copied.

In the FOR command, the slash is used to separate functions.

## Percent Sign

This symbol is often used when creating batch files. Percent signs are used to replace the name of a made-up variable or parameter with the data contained by the same variable or parameter.

Made-up parameters range from digits 0 to 9 depending on the name of the batch file. For instance, %5 will be substituted by the fifth value in the batch file. If there are less than five values in the batch file, the parameter simply disappears displaying no error prompt.

## Double Quote

Enclosing a double quote in a command line tells the interpreter to disable parsing the command until another double quote is encountered in the same line. The group of letters, words, characters or numbers will thus be considered as a single item. For example:

```
A:\>Batch1.bat 9 " 8 7 " 6 " 5 4 3 "
```

This interpreter creates dummy parameters where the first value is the digit 9, the second value is the string 8 7, the third value is the digit 4 and the last value is the string 5 4 3.

Empty pairs of double quotes are construed as void signals. Often, DOS commands simply ignore the pair unless it will affect the parsing of a command line especially when you are using SET, IF and ECHO command.

## Square Brackets

Data packets enclosed by square brackets ([ ]) are executed by IO.SYS and DEBUG.EXE as a primary reference to operands.

Be careful when using square brackets as DOS has two reserved words surrounded by square brackets: [Menu] and [Common], which are both executed by the CONFIG.SYS interpreter. [Menu] represents a subset of other commands like SUBMENU, MENUITEM, MENUDEFAULT and MENUCOLOR.

## Colon

How the interpreter recognizes a colon (:) hinges on its position in a command line. In batch files, if a colon is placed at the beginning of a line, it interprets the succeeding word as a label. If there are other succeeding words, the interpreter will only recognize the first one while ignoring the rest.

Double colons (::) placed as the first two characters of a command line disable the operation of the same line.

Colons placed after a letter in the command line sets the preceding letter as the address of the directory. For example:

```
B:

B:\

B:\WINDOWS\
```

makes disk B: the default disk.

## Left and Right Arrow

The two directional arrows ( < ) and ( > ) redirects the operations performed by the COMMAND.COM interpreter. Depending on the direction of the arrow, the interpreter links the command to a data source. For instance:

```
MORE < B:\WINDOWS\Sampler.txt
```

The utility filter MORE.COM obtains the data from the B:\WINDOWS directory, which, in this case, is the data from the text file Sampler.txt. Consider this example:

14

```
COPY /? > Sampler2.txt
```

The interpreter will first perform the COPY command but instead of displaying the copied information on screen, the right arrow redirects the result of the COPY command and stores it inside the text file, Sampler2.txt.

Aside from files, ports (COM1, COM2, COM3, LPT1 and LPT2 to name a few) can also be used as a data resource.

## Double Right Arrow

Similar to the single Right Arrow, the Double Right Arrow ( >> ) also signals redirection of output. While Right Arrow wipes out the data of the target file and replaces its contents with the output of a command on the arrow's left side, Double Right Arrows preserve the contents of the target file and just append its data with the output of a command on the double arrow's left.

## Pipe or Vertical Bar

The pipe separator is another kind of redirector as it transfers data information from one utility to another. The only difference this redirector has compared to the arrow redirectors is that COMMAND.COM interpreter makes a temporary target file whenever you use a pipe separator.

15

# Chapter 3: The Most Basic DOS Commands

The commands listed in this section are the most commonly-used (and arguably, the most important) DOS commands. There's no need to memorize these commands because merely understanding how each command functions can already help you when coding simple DOS programs.

### Directory

Similar to a book's table of contents, the directory stores and compiles the following data:

- Filenames
- File extensions
- File size
- Date and time of the file's last update

To access this command, simply type the command `dir` and hit the Enter key. This will list down all the directories stored in your computer, complete with all the helpful details about each directory. Note that at the last part of this listing, there will be a line showing how much free space is remaining on your hard disk.

### Scrolling through the Directory

When the directory command is used, the files are listed vertically on the screen. Most of the time, you will find the list hard to read since most modern computers already have hundreds, maybe even thousands, of files stored in them. Holding down the **CTRL (Control) key + S** will allow you to stop the listing from loading other files allowing you to view loaded filenames more closely. When finished, you can hit the spacebar to allow the listing to continue.

If you need to enter a new command after this, you need to go back to the `C:\>` prompt.

### Pausing through the directory listing

The "pause" command can be added to the `DIR` so you can view the directory a screen at a time.

To do this, simply type:

```
dir/p
```

on the command line and hit Enter. After the list fills up the whole length of the screen, it will discontinue listing files. When this happens, simply hit the spacebar if you want to continue to the next screen. You can continue doing this until you go back to the command prompt.

## Splitting the view into five columns

For a quick view of the files, you may split the screen into five different columns. Simply type the command:

```
dir/w
```

("w" stands for "wide"), then press Enter. This will prompt DOS to list just the filenames and their corresponding extension on the monitor.

## Printing the Directory Listing

You may also instruct DOS to send data to your printer, thereby printing the files listed in the directory. Simply type the command:

```
dir > prn
```

then hit the Enter key. As discussed in the preceding chapter the right arrow ( > ) signals output redirection, only in this case the output is sent to prn refers to "printer". Also, you can also print out a "wide" view of the files by typing the command:

```
dir/w > prn.
```

## Checking for a lone file

If you would like to locate or check just one file, you may do so by typing the filename right after the DIR line. To look for a file with the name samplefile.txt, type:

```
dir samplefile.txt
```

(using the filename.extension format) after the C:\> prompt, then press the Enter key. This will cause the screen to either list the file itself or display a "file not found" prompt if no such file

17

exists within the database.

### Checking for a group of documents

The apostrophe ( * ) symbol is defined as a "wildcard", serving as a substitute for any character (or set of characters). This can be helpful if the programmer wants to list all files starting with a specific letter or a group of letters.

To use the wildcard feature in, say, looking for all files that start with the letter "F", simply type:

```
dir f*
```

and hit the Enter key. To add another set of filenames, simply hit the F3 key (this is the "recall" feature, which will be discussed in the succeeding chapter), backspace twice, then exchange the letter F for another letter.

You may also use the * feature to list all documents having the same extension. To look for all documents with the .txt extension, simply type:

```
dir *.txt
```

and press Enter. You can then recall the command and then change the extension with a new one to list down files bearing the same extension as the new one.

### Recall a DOS Command

As mentioned above, pressing F3 can be used to recall the last command you entered. By pressing the up arrow key on your keyboard, you can also scroll through previously entered commands. The command can then be edited so the variables can be changed as needed.

### Clearing the Screen

If the screen is already filled with output data, you can clear it by typing:

```
CLS
```

This command leaves a blank screen for you to work with.

## Creating a DOS File

File can also be created easily using DOS. For example, if you want to create a letter (with the .ltr extension) addressed to your colleague. Simply type:

```
copy con Letter.ltr
```

and hit the Enter key. This will prompt DOS to create a new file bearing the .ltr extension. In order to create content for the file, simply type in the content and hit the F6 function key. Press Enter to finish.

After this, DOS will give you a message saying:

```
1 File(s) has been copied
```

To double-check the file, simply search for the file in the directory using:

```
dir l*
```

## Copying a File

This helpful command that can be used to copy the content of one file into another. As an example, to copy the letter you made in the previouse into another file, simply type:

```
copy Letter.ltr Letter2.ltr
```

after the C:\> prompt, then hit the Enter key. This will give a message that file was successfully replicated, and then creates a new file (Letter2.ltr) bearing the contents of the original file (Letter.ltr).

Keep in mind that filenames should not be more than eight characters in length, and file extensions are always no more than three characters in length.

The versatility of the copy command is that the command alone can be used to print through DOS: simply type:

```
copy Letter.ltr prn
```

and hit the Enter key to print out the contents of your letter.

### Copying a File with a New Extension

If you are unable to find a program that opens file with the .ltr extension, you might want to convert your letter into a more universal text file. This can also be handled by DOS by using the same copy command: simply type:

```
copy Letter.ltr Letter.txt
```

and hit the Enter key. Checking the directory, you should be able to see a new file this time with the .txt extension.

### Checking a File with DOS

If you want to re-check the contents of the letter using DOS, simply type:

```
type Letter.txt
```

and hit the Enter key. This prints the contents of the file on-screen. Remember, however, that this should not be used with `.com`, `.sys`, `.exe`, and `.bas` extensions, since these were meant to activate programs. Printing these on the screen will only display gibberish.

### Renaming a File

To rename your letter, simply type:

```
ren Letter.txt Hello.txt
```

and hit the Enter key. This will change the `Letter.txt` file into one entitle `Hello.txt`.

### Renaming a Group of Files

Using the wildcard (*) character discussed earlier, you can rename an entire group of files. For example, if you want to rename all files with the `.ltr` extension into `.txt`, you can simply type:

```
ren *.ltr *.txt
```

and press the Enter Key. Or, you can also rename files with the same name but with different extensions: `ren file.* newfile.*` and then Enter.

# Chapter 4: Internal DOS Commands

Aside from the commands listed in the previous chapter, DOS uses internal command instructions executed by the interpreter. Unlike other utility objects, the command interpreter is permanently installed in the DOS memory allowing efficient execution of data and response. What differentiates internal DOS commands from other command types is that the execution of instructions does not return error codes that may complicate your program flow.

### Short Help

One of the most interesting characteristic of DOS commands is its being user-friendly. If you don't understand how a certain command works, the COMMAND.COM interpreter will help you by displaying a short definition of the command. Help texts can be accessed by typing the command followed by "/?". For instance, you want to know what the command BREAK does, you can enter the following in your command prompt:

```
BREAK /?
```

DOS will immediately respond by displaying this help text:

```
BREAK - disk access intercept control
```

The only disadvantage of the help text that DOS provides is that they are either too short or too technical for a beginner to understand. In the succeeding sections, this chapter will include the help text provided by DOS for each command including a detailed definition of how each command works and corresponding examples.

### Break

(Help text: disk access intercept control)

The BREAK command instructs DOS to prompt whenever it detects a user pressing a CTRL + C or CTRL + Break command to intercept the file listing. If you want DOS to issue an advisory prompt, enter:

BREAK ON

21

If you want to check the current BREAK setting (if it is turned on), enter:

BREAK

## CD

(Help text: <code>change directory</code>)

This command is self-explanatory as it enables you to switch the present directory on any disk in the system using a specific path. For instance if you enter:

<code>CD : A:\Windows</code>

This command will set the present directory to `\Windows` provided the present default disk is not `A:\`. Other ways to use the command `CD` are:

| | |
|---|---|
| `CD \` | Root directory |
| `CD ..` | Parent directory |
| `CD ..\..` | Primary level subdirectory |
| `CD ..\..\..` | Secondary level subdirectory |

If a `CD` command is used without specifying the pathname, then it merely changes the current directory to a specified disk.

## CHCP

(Help text: <code>change code page</code>)

`Codepage` is a selection of symbols and characters used a library to print messages on your screen. When using CHCP command without specifying the `codepage` number of the desired character set, DOS will simply display the current `codepage` number.

Unless you have installed an `NLSFUNC.EXE` driver which contains the `codepage` for the character sets of various foreign languages, you can't use the CHCP command. For instance if you have loaded `codepage 720` for Arabic and `codepage 737` for Greek, then using command `CHCP 720` switches the current `codepage` to Arabic while command `CHCP 737` switches the current `codepage` to Greek.

Other codepage identifiers are:

| Identifier | Character |
|------------|-----------|
| 437 | OEM – United States |
| 720 | Arabic |
| 850 | Latin |
| 862 | Hebrew |
| 936 | Chinese (simplified) |
| 1141 | German |
| 1147 | French |
| 10001 | Japanese |
| 10003 | Korean |
| 10002 | Chinese |
| 10021 | Thai |

## CTTY

(Help text: `redirection of I/O links`)

Under the CTTY commands, the three command settings that manage the input-output channels include: STDERR, STDIN, and STDOUT. All devices are linked to the computer through the console CON devices - the mouse and keyboard for input, and monitor display for output. Aside from just the CON device, CTTY accepts information from the following command ports: LPT1 (PRN), LPT2, COM1 (AUX), COM2, COM3 and even the virtual NUL device.

CTTY prevents accidental disruption of execution. It also prevents unwanted error prompt that can't be redirected to a different DOS channel. Consider this batch file:

```
@ctty lpt1
copy /A Sample.txt Sample2.txt
echo Input any letter or number to exit > con
pause < con
```

```
ctty con
```

In the above example, notice that the instructions of the COPY command will only result to an error message, which will not be displayed on-screen thanks to the CTTY command. The echo command which requires the user to "Input any letter or number to exit" will be displayed as the right arrow ( > ) directs the instruction to the console CON device. The instructions in the PAUSE command is directly linked by the left arrow ( < ) to the input console CON device which, in this case, pertains to the keyboard.

**Date**

(Help text: date display and reset)

The command DATE allows you to set a new date. If you don't specify a date in the command, the current date will be displayed. For instance, if the current date in the DOS system is July 14, 2015, simply supplying this:

```
DATE
```

will give you an output that looks like this:

```
14.07.2015
```

If you use this command:

```
DATE 13.07.2015
```

then you are resetting the system date to July 13, 2015 instead.

**DEL**

(Help text: file(s) deletion)

The delete DEL command allows you to disable the file specification within the directory path. In other words, DEL command does not wipe the command off the memory; instead these files occupy slots for invalid entries until they are finally overwritten by a different file. This gives you a chance to recover "deleted" files by using the UNDELETE.EXE utility.

Consider the following command line:

```
DEL C:\DOS\DeleteMe.txt /P
```

In the above example:

| | |
|---|---|
| `C:\DOS\` | The disk and path that holds the file to be deleted. If this is left blank, then it is implied that the current directory will be deleted. |
| `DeleteMe.txt` | The filename of the file to be deleted. |
| `/P` | In case you coded the wrong information, this parameter will instruct DOS to ask for a secondary confirmation via a prompt before DOS carries out file deletion. |

The `ERASE` command functions the same way as the `DEL` command.

**For**

(Help text: `cycle operator`)

This operator arranges a loop execution of a combination of various commands. For instance if you want to run a code that displays three different image files: `sample1.gif`, `sample2.jpg` and `sample3.png`.

Instead of using three separate command lines to display the above files, the `FOR` command allows you to perform the same command three times in just a single command line:

```
FOR %A IN (sample1 sample2 sample3) DO TYPE %A
                (.gif .jpg .png)
```

In the above example:

| | |
|---|---|
| `IN` | This reserve word that assigns the values inside the parenthesis to the variable for every loop. Each value can be separated by separators including spaces as in this example. |
| `DO` | This reserve word introduces the command that will be looped depending on the number of variable inside the parentheses. |

In every cycle, a value will be assigned to the variable before the command TYPE evaluates the expression.

%A        This is a cycle variable comprised by the percent sign and a single-letter name.

## GOTO

(Help text: `jump to a label`)

This command instructs the interpreter to initiate a jump to a label, which should be defined in one of the lines within the batch file. Labels are defined by affixing a colon followed by a temporary label. Once the label is defined, the `GOTO` command should be supplied with the same name; otherwise, the batch file won't be able to perform the jump. The name of the label can exceed eight characters but only the first eight characters must be added next to the `GOTO` command.

To illustrate how this command works, assuming you labelled a command certain command line as `:JULY14`, the command that tells DOS to jump to said line is:

`GOTO JULY14`

If there are two lines with the same `:JULY14` label, the interpreter won't proceed with the jump so be careful when labeling lines. For instance if you have another line defined as `:MTHLINE14` which accounts for nine characters, when instructing DOS to jump to said line, write this:

`GOTO MTHLINE1`

Notice that in the above example, we omitted the character 4 because `GOTO` command only considers the first eight characters.

## IF

(Help text: `condition operator`)

If you were used to using IF in other programming language then you would not find it hard to use IF inn DOS. Condition operators in DOS perform only three kinds of conditional checks, which are ERRORLEVEL check, equality check and existence check.

- ERRORLEVEL Check

    After the interpreter evaluates the command by execution of DOS utilities, the interpreter may send an ERRORLEVEL, which merely serves as a notification if the interpreter was able to process your instructions or not. If it failed to carry out your command, ERRORLEVEL will enumerate the details on what possibly went wrong in the command.

    It computes a decimal value between 0 and 255. Obviously, a 0 ERROR LEVEL meant that the command was evaluated successfully. Now to perform an ERRORLEVEL check, consider the following:

    ```
    IF ERRORLEVEL 0 ECHO Evaluation of command
    was successful

    IF NOT ERRORLEVEL 0 ECHO Evaluation of
    command has failed.
    ```

    In this example, if the ERRORLEVEL gives a value of 0 then it displays this response: Evaluation of command was successful. Otherwise, it will give a different response saying that the Evaluation of command has failed.

- EQUALITY Check

    The equality check allows you to compare two words or the values that they represent. Separate them by a double equal sign ( ==). Equality conditions use dummy parameters or the values represented by variables and depending on the result of the check, a command instruction will be executed. Consider this example:

    ```
    ECHO OFF
    IF NOT Y==%2 GOTO VAL14
    ECHO   Enter   a   parameter   value   after
    evaluation
    GOTO END14
    :VAL14
    ```

27

```
ECHO The parameter value is[%2]
:END14
```

The initial line of the above batch file performs a check that determines whether the user has entered a parameter in the command line. It then evaluates whether the input parameter has the same value as the second string. If the input value does not match with the string then it affirms the condition that the Y does not equate to %2 symbol prompting the command GOTO VAL14 to be executed thus executing the line labeled VAL14, which in this case displays this response: The parameter value is including your input value.

If the IF NOT condition returns a false value then this means that there are no input value. If this is the case, the interpreter will execute the GOTO END14 command line instead, prompting the program to end.

- EXISTENCE **Check**

  Usually performed on directories, logical utilities and files, existence checks (IF EXIST) determine whether these objects, well, exists. Simultaneously, the absence condition (IF NOT EXIST) check determines if an object does not exist. For instance:

  ```
  ECHO OFF
  IF NOT EXIST Sample1.txt GOTO PRINT
  ECHO The text file Sample1.txt is in this
  directory
  GOTO END14
  :PRINT
  ECHO The file Sample1.txt is not in this
  directory.
  ECHO The file must be in a different
  directory
  :END14
  ```

In the above batch file, the program evaluates if the file named Sample1.txt does not exist within the search directory. If no such file exists then the IF NOT EXIST condition is fulfilled, then the interpreter will have to execute the GOTO PRINT command. The program then evaluates the command line labelled PRINT, which in this case displays the message: The file Sample1.txt is not in this directory. It will also display another message: The file must be in a different directory but on a different line.

If the file does exist then the IF NOT EXIST condition is not fulfilled thereby displaying this message: The text file Sample1.txt is in this directory and then proceed to executing the GOTO END14 command that terminates the program.

**LFNFOR**

(Help text: long filenames display mode)

While DOS generally allows filenames up to eight characters but this is mainly due to the LFNFOR command is OFF by default. In other words, unless the LFNFOR command is turned ON, long filenames will be truncated to just eight characters discarding the rest.

Using the LFNFOR command only determines if the long filename display setting is turned on. If you want to turn on the setting, enter the following:

LFNFOR ON

in the command prompt. If you want to turn it off, just enter the following:

LFNFOR OFF

**MD**

(Help text: make directory)

This command is self-explanatory as it enables you to make a new directory. Consider this example:

MD A:\WINDOWS\COLLECT

In the above command line:

A:\WINDOWS\ is the pathname of an existing directory and the location where the new command line will be created.

COLLECT is the name of the directory that the above command line creates

A similar command that can be used interchangeably with the MD command is the MKDIR command.

**PATH**

(Help text: search path(s) specification)

This command sets a defined path when searching for programs within the various DOS directories. While the SET command has almost the same function as the PATH command, the latter changes the characters of the new path to uppercase. The PATH command line should be accompanied by one or more already existing paths, each isolated by semicolons. Consider the following examples:

PATH A:\WINDOWS\XYX; A:\WINDOWS\XYY;A:\WINDOWS\YXX

Interpreters tend not to evaluate a path command that ends with a semicolon separator.

**Pause**

(Help text: temporary stop)

If the interpreter encounters a line that includes the PAUSE command, it will temporarily halt the command. It will then display the following message: "Press any key to continue..."

If the user is wiser, he can stop the execution of the rest of the program by using any of the following combinations: CTRL + C; CTRL + BREAK and ALT + 03.

Consider the following command lines:

ECHO Δ | PAUSE > NIL    In this command line, instead of just delaying the execution of the program, when the user inputs the Δ character, the program ends

|  |  |
|---|---|
|  | execution at once and without a slight break. |
| PAUSE < CON | Instead of displaying a delay message, the execution is transported away from the input console. This is similar to the CTTY NUL redirection. |
| PAUSE > NUL | Unless an ECHO command is turned on, DOS will not display the PAUSE message. |

## Prompt

(Help text: prompt specification)

The PROMPT command assigns the values included in the inherent variables stored in the system. There are times when data can't be written directly to the program as the interpreter might have other ways to interpret them as a reserved symbol. This is usually used if you just need to print the character as it is. For instance:

| $Q | Equal Symbol (=) |
|---|---|
| $$ | Single Dollar sign ($) |
| $T | Current Time |
| $D | Current Date |
| $P | Current Path or Current Directory |
| $N | Current Letter Name of Disk |
| $G | Greater-Than symbol or Right Arrow |
| $L | Less-Than symbol or Left Arrow |
| $B | Pipe sign or Vertical Bar |

## RD

(Help text: remove directory)

If the following conditions are satisfied: (a) the directory to be removed is not a root directory, (b) directory is located on a writable disk location, (c) directory does not contain any file and (d) not the current directory, then you can use the RD command to erase a directory. Consider this example:

RD E:\TEMP\SAMPLEDIR

In the following example the:

SAMPLEDIR is the directory that will be erased

E:\TEMP\ Pathname of the directory that will be erased. Take note that only the last directory name in the address will be deleted. In this example, TEMP\ directory will not be deleted.

**Time**

(Help text: time display and reset)

Almost the same as how the DATE command works. When determining what the system deems as the current time, you can just type the command TIME. If you want to reset the time to a new one, type the command TIME followed by the new time. For instance:

TIME 12:13:59,47

sets the current time to 12:13:59,47 following this format:

HH:MM:SS,hh

Where the HH (hours), MM (minutes) and SS (seconds) are separated by colons while the hundredths or fraction of a second is specified by a comma preceding it. This format is not set in stone as it may vary depending on the activated COUNTRY command.

# Chapter 5: Configuration Commands

DOS owes its configuration from three non-formatted system files that should be stored within the root directory of the main disk that holds the DOS files. These system files are AUTOEXEC.BAT, CONFIG.SYS and MSDOS.SYS. Among the three commands, CONFIG.SYS enjoys the longest history with the DOS systems.

Every command line included in the CONFIG.SYS system files instructs one of the main interpreters (IO.SYS) to load the system while COMMAND.COM carries out the execution of the command. Other commands and syntax are included within the CONFIG.SYS file.

Several commands within CONFIG.SYS may not have an equivalent in the later versions of DOS but most of them survived to be included in the recognizable commands executed by COMMAND.COM.

**ACCDATE**

(Help text: registration of last access date)

This command determined which drives would display their last access dates. For example:

```
ACCDATE A- B+ C+ D- E+
```

A-   The plus ( + ) sign that accompanied the letter A means that the you are disallowing Disk A from displaying their last access dates.

B+   The minus ( – ) sign that accompanied the letter B means that the you are allowing Disk B from displaying their last access dates.

C+   Same as B.

D-   Same as A.

E+   Same as B and C.

**BUFFERS**

(Help text: number of buffers)

This command saves a memory space for a buffer that's usually occupies 512 bytes worth of memory to prevent the disks from crashing. Unless you set a different number for your buffers, DOS has 30 initial buffers and 0 secondary buffers.

This buffer command allows you to create 1 – 90 initial buffers and 0 – 8 secondary buffers. For example:

BUFFERS=90,8

creates 90 initial buffers and 8 secondary buffers which are the maximum values for each buffer. If the initial buffer level is set to a number less than 30, some functions might be executed at a slower pace.

### COUNTRY

(Help text: loading national adaptation data)

This command activates the data from COUNTRY.SYS system file and loads them into the DOS data tables to integrate the rules and variables to match a country. This also turns on special language characters for files and directories and their contents.

### DEVICE

(Help text: loading a device driver)

This command loads various drivers that are externally installed in the system. This gives the files from these drivers a special header for execution.

### EXIT

(Help text: closure of current interpreter session)

This command ends all the current activities performed within the module. It frees the memory from any activity. Although DOS allows various program modules to run in the same memory bit, the parent program sometimes slows down and become inaccessible. If this happens, you can use the EXIT command to stop all the running processes in the system.

## LOCK

(Help text: `forbid concurrent access`)

Various programs contain crucial data and information that can effect several DOS program. If there are other users using your computer then it is better to LOCK some commands interpreted by the COMMAND.COM interpreter to allow only restricted access. For instance, if you don't want anyone restoring your deleted files then you can LOCK the UNDELETE.EXE utility.

The locked state of utilities can be undone by using the UNLOCK command.

## SHELL

(Help text: `interpreter shell specification`)

This command loads an .exe file without returning the control back to the IO.SYS interpreter. This is usually the last command evaluated in the system because CONFIG.SYS prefers to execute the commands through COMMAND.COM before jumping to a different interpreter. If the shell command is not available in the CONFIG.SYS system files, the command interpreter goes back to the current disk.

# Chapter 6: Writing Batch Files

One of the strong suites of DOS programming -- one that leverages its straightforwardness and ease of use -- is in the creation of Batch Files. These files are so called because they are essentially sets of instructions that can allow Windows users to do a large number of things as quickly and as efficiently as possible. They are like small bits of programming code, but you don't have to be a full-fledged programmer to create them.

Batch files can be thought of as a combination of both basic and internal DOS commands that were discussed in the previous chapters. These sets of command lines can manage a variety of files, and can be used to easily delete the Internet cache, browsing history, browser cookies and other temp files with just a click of a mouse. And because it's DOS, everything runs smoothly and more efficiently than other methods.

When writing batch files, however, one must remember that some DOS commands work in certain versions but may be useless in others. For example, the command `deltree` is available in Win 98's DOS, but not in XP. Due to this, the programmer must make sure that the commands used in the batch are compatible with the implementing system.

In this section, you will be taken through a tutorial allowing you to access a simple OS-like environment. This will essentially be a batch file capable of showing different menus, as well as displaying the different options contained. This can be used for different purposes, such as letting the user select which DOS game they wish to play.

**Important Note:** If you are using slightly-modern Windows OS versions (Windows XP or higher), some of the command lines in this book would not work. The programmer could work on a device running either Win 98 or just plain DOS, or you may also use any preferred emulator available online.

To start, simply go to your Notepad, or open up the Editor if you're already on DOS (simply type `edit` at the DOS command prompt). For those using Notepad, remember to save under the proper file extension -- your menu might be saved with a `.bat.txt` extension, which will return an error.

In the tutorial, you will learn different DOS commands: `echo`, `choice`, `cls`, `labels`, `if`, and `errorlevels`.

## Echo

The use of this command can have different objectives: it can be used to hide all commands used (so the end-user does not see), and it can also be used to show custom messages. We will be using this for both in our setup. To start, this will be the first line of code:

### *Echo off*

This tells the DOS that the commands to be used from this point forward are not to be shown. However, it does not work on itself (the user will still see the `echo off` line), so you will have to clear that manually. The next line of code will hence be:

### *Cls*

Or, you can also use `@echo off` so you can proceed without having to type `cls`. Now, in order to provide a customized message, we will use the echo command again:

```
Echo Say Hi to my DOS operating system!
```

Take note that this is a little simpler than most programming languages, as you won't need any quotation marks around the actual message.

After this simple line, you could test your code. Save it and then start it up -- on any Windows system, simply find the file with the .bat extension and double-click it. There are some instances when it will open and then close straightaway -- in this case, simply pull up the DOS prompt (located in the Start Menu, filed under the Accessories folder). You can also add a Pause line at the last part of the program.

If you are on DOS, simply exit the editor and type the filename at the `C:\>` prompt. Hit Enter afterwards. Remember that you have to include the `.bat` extension when looking for the file, as DOS will know that by itself.

If you typed in `Pause` as mentioned, you would see that your

37

program will sport the words Press any key to continue, just like any classic arcade game!

## Labels, Errorlevels, If, and Choice

The Choice line will give the user program users the ability to choose the activity the program will do. The If line, on the other hand, gives the program instructions on what it needs to do given a specific option has been selected. The Errorlevel line is essential in helping the program make this decision, and finally, Label will serve as the markers for places in the program one can move to any time.

These four elements are essential in giving a navigational interface for our little program. When combines, it allows the user to move at will from one option to another.

To demonstrate how this works, remove the Pause line that was placed earlier then enter the following line of code in its place:

```
Echo Select the number of the game you want to
play.
Echo 1. Solitaire
Echo 2. Pinball
Echo 3. Minesweeper
Echo x. Close the program
Choice /c:123x
If errorlevel 4 goto exit
If errorlevel 3 goto minesweeper
If errorlevel 2 goto pinball
If errorlevel 1 goto solitaire

:solitaire
Echo Solitaire will now run.
Pause
Goto start

:pinball
Echo Pinball will run now.
Pause
Goto start

:minesweeper
```

```
Echo Minesweeper will run now.
Pause
Goto start

:exit
```

Then, add this code at the program's very top:

```
:start
```

Now, run the program to see how it is doing. You can actually try selecting 1, 2, 3, or x (to close) to see if it will work.

You would notice that the code utilized the Echo line in the command to give the user some choice of programs. This is not required for the choice command to work, in reality -- but to make a user-friendly program, the user would need to know what options they have. In other words, the information is not needed before the choice line will work.

Now, we will also look at the line of code that is connected to this command:

```
Choice /c:123x
```

In this example, `Choice` will be the name of the command, but the program needs to be instructed about the options that the program user can choose from. To perform this task, the command line parameters are used. The "`/c`" is typed to invoke a "C switch" (more on this later), and then the : (colon) which is followed by the choices. Later on, we will also discuss the other switch types available.

The program will then have to be told what it will do when the program user selects an option. The Choice part handles this for us, since it essentially "pauses" the program's execution until the user hits a button. In this sense, the programmer need not worry about knowing when this happens.

The `If` segments in the code will tell the program what it needs to do. In layman's terms, it will be like "When the user selects the fourth option, proceed to the exit label. If he selects the third, proceed to the minesweeper label...", etc.

You may have noticed that these options are listed from the very last to the first -- this is a required thing when doing batch files. The programmer should never list options from first to last.

Also, you would notice that in coding `exit`, we called it `errorlevel 4` instead of `errorlevel x` (after the letter that was used for the options). This is because with `Errorlevels`, the exact key is not used -- instead, it is the option number (the $4^{th}$, in this case) that is recognized by the system.

Next, we have the `Goto` line, which will tell the program to `jump` or `goto` another part in that program. The words after it, which is its label, will tell the program where it should land.

The line that says, ":`pinball`" defines the label. When the program reads "`goto pinball`", it is essentially telling the DOS program to perform the task after "`:pinball`". Next up is a message that tells the user that the game Pinball will now launch. If above code is not a simple demo, the programmer can include the code to run Pinball in the program lines

After this, add the "`Press any key to continue...`" message before we include the program code "`goto start`". When the program user hits any keys, the code will begin searching for the location of the line "`:start`", which is placed at the start of the code. This effectively creates a loop, having the code repeat from the start (main menu) when a key is pressed.

# Chapter 7: Building on the Choice Command

This chapter is a technical continuation to the earlier one. This will build upon the skills and concept we discussed earlier. Just like before, open up Notepad if you are running Windows, and open up the MS-DOS editor if you are on DOS (simply type the word "edit" at the command prompt, then hit Enter). Before beginning, save the file and call it "choice.bat". If you are on Notepad, make sure that the "All Files" option is selected. Otherwise, the program might end with a ".bat.txt" extension that will not open correctly.

Remember that earlier we used the "C switch", which lets the programmer decide which options the user of the program will choose from. There are also other options available in the C switch's place -- N, S, T, and "prompt text". Remember that if nothing is assumed in place of the C switch, the choice will assume that the programmer is just asking a Yes/No question. In this case, the options will only be yes or no.

## N Switch

The next switch we will look at is "N". Upon using C switch, we commanded the program to give the user a program similar to this:

[1,2,3,x]?

It will basically be there to remind the user what options they have, in addition to the contents of the echo command. However, if the programmer does not want to show this to the program user, the N switch can be used. Hence, the code will look like this:

Choice /c:123x /n

In this case, all the user will see will be the flashing DOS prompt (which is the flashing underscore) and the user's decision will be dependent on the options given them.

## S Switch

The next switch we will use is the S switch, which can be appended in the following code:

Choice /c:123x /n /s

All this switch does is to treat the keys pressed as a case-sensitive item. This is much like when you are typing a password into the prompt of a webpage -- if the letters were capitalized when they weren't supposed to be, then the password would not be accepted. Likewise, if you use the capital letter X when exiting, for example, then the code will beep you -- since it does not recognize X, only the smaller x.

The S switch can be significant because it allows the programmer to create a different result when lowercase and uppercase letters are pressed.

**T Switch**

The T-switch is basically a timer switch, which will have the Choice automatically choose an option on behalf of the user, if they will not enter anything before the timer expires. The following syntax will then be used:

Choice /c:123x /n /s /t:x, 30

Before we explain this, note that you do not have to use every switch like we are doing, since this is done only to build in top of what we already know. Also, these switches do not have to be in the same order enter (except for the "prompt text" option which will be discussed a little later).

As you may have noticed, there are two other elements after the T switch -- the option it will choose automatically, and the time it will take before that is selected. This can be changed to any value, but do not forget the colon (:) and the coma (,) so that DOS can clearly understand what you mean.

**Prompt Text**

You can also always use the "prompt text" option, which allows you to display a line of text. Of course, the Echo command discussed earlier can always be used -- except that "prompt text" takes a little less time.

All you will have to do is to enter the text that you wish to be displayed, on the same line as the original Choice command. However, make sure that this is done after any switches that have been used previously:

Choice /c:123x /n /s /t:x,30 Choose an option

# Chapter 8: Selected Utilities

DOS Interpreters executes coded instruction in the form of command lines or batch files based on the syntactical arrangement of reserved words, characters, commands, strings and variables. As the popularity of DOS as a programming tool rose mainly due to the release of relatively newer Windows OS, several utilities were supplied to enhance the inherent functions of each command interpreters.

The makers of DOS understood that introducing new utilities might hamper how the users understood the commands already included in DOS. The programmers behind DOS devised a way to help DOS users understand how each utility works in the same manner that users come to understand how each command works. Help texts can be accessed by adding the /? parameter after the utility name, for instance: if you want to know what the utility Edit.com is, just key in the following in your command prompt:

```
EDIT.COM /?
```

This request will prompt DOS to display a help text about EDIT.COM.

Some utilities may require a specific DOS version number so after the utility is installed, it may ask DOS to return a response corresponding to its version number. If the number does not match the number the utility requires, then DOS will not be able to process functions supplied by the utility.

The utilities that are particular with version numbers are:

- Sort.exe
- Mem.exe
- Fc.exe
- Command.com
- Doskey.com
- Find.exe
- Format.com
- Chkdsk.exe
- Debug.exe
- Attrib.exe
- Diskcopy.exe
- Label.exe

**ATTRIB.EXE**

(Help text: `attribute changing utility`)

When stored inside directories, each files has a corresponding record. This utility can change the status of the files including which users are granted access.    In this example:

`Attrib.exe +H +A A:\WINDOWS\NOTES\Sample1.txt /S`

`+H +A`                                              These letters correspond to certain attributes that this utility assigns to the file status. Each letter corresponds to a file setting

- `A` – archiving
- `H` – hidden status
- `R` – read-only status
- `S` – viewable within the system

The signs that precede the letter correspond to what to make of the attribute. The plus sign (+) sets the attribute while the minus sign (–) removes the attribute from the file.

In the above example, the text file Sample.txt is not only hidden (+H) but also archived (+A). This utility also assumes that unmentioned attributes remain as is.

`A:\WINDOWS\NOTES\Sample1.txt` This is the pathname and the filename of the files being processed by the utility.    If    the

45

/S                                                    pathname is not supplied then it is implied that it refers to files in the current directory.

/S                                                    This parameter continues to locate other similar files within the subdirectory.

## CHKDSK.EXE

(Help text: disks checking tool)

If you owned a portable storage device like memory card, external hard drive and flash drives, the successors to the throne once held by compact disks and diskettes, you would have come across the term FAT or the File Allocation Tables. They occupy memory spaces without adding real value to the system. What CHKDSK.EXE does is that it compares FAT tables stored in various systems (FAT32, FAT16 and FAT 12) to disclose similar links and lost files. Once the utility is done performing a check within the system, it gives out a summary of its findings.

If the CHKDSK.EXE is evaluated in the command line without any parameters or pathnames, the utility will understand that you are implying a command that checks on the current directory instead of FAT tables. In this example:

```
Chkdsk.exe A: /V /F
```

A:    The pathname where a disk check will be performed.

/V    The parameter that instructs the CHKDSK.EXE to list down all the names of the files processed in the path.

/F    The parameter that instructs the same utility to fix the error found in each file.

The SCANDISK.EXE performs all the disk checks done by CHKDSK.EXE however aside from this, the former performs extra performance check. CHKDSK.EXE is only useful as it displays full information of the series of checks it did.

## COMMAND.COM

(Help text: command interpreter)

This is one of the three resident program utilities mentioned in Chapter 2. It is responsible for the evaluation of commands in the command line and in batch files. This utility executes all the commands in Chapter 2 and 3.

Unlike other utilities, COMMAND.COM does not leave a Program Segment Prefix (PSP) trace to the parent utility's PSP preserving the integrity of the parent utility. In other words, COMMAND.COM protects DOS by disallowing access to the main control unit that controls all the systems in DOS including COMMAND.COM. After this, COMMAND.COM carries out the instruction encoded in the command line, it loads a child module to relieve the parent utility of the previous process performed.

Consider this example:

```
COMMAND.COM A:\WINDOWS\ CON /E:1024 /L:1008 /U:225
             /Y /K B:\Example.bat
```

|  |  |
|---|---|
| A:\WINDOWS\ | This the pathname of the file that will be used to compute for a new value of the variable %COMSPEC% which creates a new child module. If the command line did not include a pathname then the value from the parent module will be given to the %COMSPEC% variable. |
| CON | This reserved word that pertains to an Input-Output module. |
| /E:1024 | This optional prescription creates an environmental variable with 1024 bytes worth of memory available. |
|  | (Allows $256 - 32768$ bytes) |

47

| | |
|---|---|
| /L:1008 | Another optional prescription that defines the size of internal buffer. The defined size must be enough to cover all the substitution process in the command line. |
| | (Allows 128 – 1024 bytes; Default: 256 bytes) |
| /U:225 | Another optional prescription that defines the size of input buffer. The defined size must be enough to cover the ceiling length of the command line prior to substitution. |
| | (Allows 128 – 255 bytes; Default: 128 bytes) |
| /Y | This parameter instructs COMMAND.COM to execute the commands of a batch file on a step-by-step basis as opposed to just giving the final output. |
| /K | This parameter announces the one-letter name of the program to be executed. |
| B:\Example.bat | The filename to be executed by COMMAND.COM |

The other parameters that COMMAND.COM utility accepts are:

| | |
|---|---|
| /MSG | This loads the ERRORLEVEL codes as a message to the memory. |
| /LOW | This instructs COMMAND.COM to use lower memory in the execution of a command. |
| /F | This option instructs the utility to proceed despite the user's input causing the preset conditions to fail. |

/Z                    This option instructs the utility to show
                      the    ERRORLEVEL    value    after
                      performing a check

## DEBUG.EXE

(Help text: debugger and mini assembler)

This special interpreter is responsible to determine the existence of errors and fix them within the coded instructions. This command interpreter is not exclusive to internal commands. For example:

Debug.exe Attrib.exe /B /S

Attrib.exe    The file that will be checked by the
              DEBUG.EXE Utility

## FIND.EXE

(Help text: word(s) searching filter)

This utility serves as a filtering device when locating for a specific text in a text file. It receives text either from user input or path redirection and then sends the results to The STDOUT or the standard output channel to display the results. To illustrate this, consider this example:

FIND /I /N " FAQ 12 " A:\WINDOWS\SRC\Drivers.txt

/I                              This    parameter
                                instructs
                                FIND.EXE
                                utility            to
                                disregard
                                whether        the
                                search string is in
                                capital letters.

/N                              This    parameter
                                instructs      the
                                utility to display
                                the    lines    with

| | |
|---|---|
| | their corresponding line numbers. |
| `" FAQ 12"` | The utility will filter files until it finds the nearest equivalent of this character string. |
| `A:\WINDOWS\SRC\Drivers.txt` | The pathname and filename of the text file into which the utility performs the string search. |

# Chapter 9: **DOS Tips and Tricks**

This chapter will not teach you to create anything, but will tell you about the different tips and tricks to make your DOS programming easier.

### Check your Memory

Running out of memory can cause your DOS program to clog up, especially if you are using a real legacy computer. Depending on the DOS and Windows versions you are using, you can perform different kinds of memory checks. Simply type "MEM/?" in order to know what kind of checks you can use.

### Customizing Directory Display

In order to set your directory listings to display in a certain way when the DIR command is used, you can change the DIRCMD variable to personalize its parameters.

In order to see all possible parameters for the DIRCMD environmental variable, simply type "DIR /?"

In order to set the DIRCMD, simply add the line "SET DIRCMD=xxxx" in the AUTOEXEC.bat file, where xxxx is the parameter you wish to use. For example, adding the "/ON" parameter would cause the results to be automatically arranged via the filename. Adding the "/W" command will automatically set the results to display in a "wide" format.

### Installing the DOSKEY

The DOSKEY is a utility that many newer OD programmers overlook, but it is one that deserves attention simply because of its powerful features. For example, with the DOSKEY installed, you could use the up arrow key to scroll through the latest DOS commands. This can greatly shorten the time needed to create a batch program.

Install DOSKEY by using a text editor (or the DOS editor) and adding the line "DOSKEY" (or "LH DOSKEY") to the end of the AUTOEXEC.BAT file. If this does not work, you will need to add a line with the full path of the DOSKEY program. For those on Windows 95, this is located at C:\WINDOWS\COMMAND directory. For those on

DOS 6.xx or earlier versions, it would most likely be at the C:\DOS directory.

Just remember that folder old systems, DOSKEY takes up a bit of memory, so remember to run a MEM check before installing it to see of you can spare some bytes.

### Backup the Config Files

Before any major changes are made (such as if you install software), always back up the AUTOEXEC.BAT as well as the CONFIG.SYS files. Software programs will usually make updates to these files without the user's permission, which can cause problems and errors to arise.

### Needing Help on a Command?

Depending on the version of DOS that is being used, you can type in the "HELP" command and the command name to get more information about it. If this does not work, you can type the command name and "/?" to receive help (e.g., DIR/?)

### Listing Every File on the Drive

This can be useful if you want to save the results as a report. Instead of going for variations of "DIR" you can use the command "CHKDSK /V" to show each file on the hard disk. As a bonus, the result will also show the total free space, total disk space, and a lot more.

In order to save this in a report so you can view it later, simply type "CHKDSK /V > DISKREPORT.TXT" (or, you can substitute "DISKREPORT.TXT" with any filename you wish.

### Shortcuts for the Copy Command

In order to copy files, the normal syntax would be:

COPY sourcepath\sourcefile destinantion\destinationfile

If currently you are browsing the source file's path, you know that you can skip that part in the command syntax. What you may not know is that the same can be done if you are already in the destination path.

### The WAIT Command in Batch Files

Perhaps you need to create a batch file that waits a number of seconds before executing. In other programming languages, that would simply be typing "WAIT", but DOS batch files do not recognize this command.If you want you want to use an analogous command, create a batch file with the following content:

@CHOICE /T:N,%1% > NUL

Save this as WAIT.BAT. In order to have your batch file to wait five seconds before executing, we just need to call the WAIT.BAT file and type the duration:

CALL WAIT 5

## Zero-Byte Placeholders

In case you have a batch file that works in many directories, you may find zero-byte placeholder files (those that only take up space in the directory but not in the hard drive) very useful. Simply use the "REM" (remark) command, and redirect the output to the filename you choose. With this, you can have the batch file put a placeholder in each directory it will act upon, leaving a trace if the batch file worked successfully or not.

## Find All Files of the Same Type

If you need to find all the files of a certain type in your hard drive, you can create a batch file for it. Simply put the following line in the batch file's content:

@dir /b /s *.%1 | more

If you want to sort the results, you can simply type "| sort" before the "| more". Save this as "FINDALL.BAT". In order to call it, you can simply type "FINDALL BAT" and it will find all the batch files on your drive. Typing "FINDALL TXT" will find all the text files, and so on.

# Conclusion

Thank you again for purchasing this book!

I hope this book was able to help you to create useful outputs using the DOS platform.

The next step is to create useful programs! DOS is remarkable for being easy to learn and use, and it can create pretty cool programs that can help you in your everyday tasks. Remember that there will always be more aspects to learn and more techniques to try out.

Finally, if you enjoyed this book, please take the time to share your thoughts and post a review on Amazon. We do our best to reach out to readers and provide the best value we can. Your positive review will help us achieve that. It'd be greatly appreciated!

Thank you and good luck!

# Check Out My Other Books

Below you'll find some of my other popular books that are popular on Amazon and Kindle as well.   Simply click on the links below to check them out.   Alternatively, you can visit my author page on Amazon to see other work done by me.

C Programming Success in a Day

Android Programming in a Day

C ++ Programming Success in a Day

Python Programming in a Day

PHP Programming Professional Made Easy

CSS Programming Professional Made Easy

Windows 8 Tips for Beginners

If the links do not work, for whatever reason, you can simply search for these titles on the Amazon website to find them.

www.ingramcontent.com/pod-product-compliance
Lightning Source LLC
Chambersburg PA
CBHW071002180526
45168CB00003B/1252